HARDPRESS.NET
HOME OF HARD-TO-FIND BOOKS

Wayside Idyls
by Henry Clinton Graves

WAYSIDE II

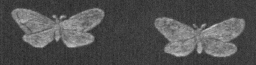

HENRY GRAV

WAYSIDE IDYLS

BY
HENRY C. GRAVES

BOSTON
SHERMAN, FRENCH & COMPANY
1913

1207

CONTENTS

CONTENTS

CONTENTS

CONTENTS

WAYSIDE IDYLS

SURSUM CORDA

Upward, hearts, towards heaven advancing,
    Christ the life has gone before.
    On the cross our sin he bore;
    In the tomb he silent lay,
    Till the resurrection day,
Victor then o'er death advancing.

Upward, hearts, the Lord ascending,
    Gives his life to dying souls;
    Sin from off their past he rolls;
    Him no bands of death can hold,
    All our ways of life unfold,
Where, behold, the Lord ascending.

Upward, hearts, no more descending.
    Here lay all earth's burdens down,
    At the tomb, near lies the crown,
    On our resurrection morn,
    It will shine in glory's dawn,
With the Lord of light descending.

Upward, hearts, in Christ confiding,
    Sorrow, care and grief assuage,
    Reading from life's daily page,

Some sweet word of promise given,
Something of the Savior risen.
Upward, hearts, in Christ confiding.

A SEA VIEW

UPON a summer scene, I view,
As in a book, I love to look—
Far off the reach of circling sea,
Hard by the shore where boat and oar
Are high and dry, while rocky cliff,
And grateful breeze invite and please;
I climb and rest upon the crest,
Where one secure may bathe at will,
Within the airy tideful deep.

The heavens above in azure sweep,
Through circling ways laden with rays,
Send forth the light in myriad beams,
That fall in sheen and glory down
On all below, all spaces fill,
All angles make, and paint the waves
In native colors, thousand hues,
Rich, changeful, changeless, opaline,
Ethereal blue, ultra marine.

A seabird poises o'er the deep,
At home in air, in ocean mist,
On sun-beat wave, in skyey flash,
I catch the glint of glittering wing;
The free firm swoop through spray and light,
Sets all my heart in pulse for flight;
And then in ranges grander far,
It soars with fancy as in play,
Beyond the watery, misty way.

Thus sunlit views fill with delight,
I am content, nor thought, nor dream,
Shall cloud for me the gladdening scene,
Here wait enwrapped in calm repose,
All doubt, all question, all complaint,
Till one sweet day is fled away;
And then, though visions change at night,
Still I shall stronger, purer be,
For wave beat cliff and vanished sea.

THRENODY ON LONGFELLOW AND EMERSON

He who for souls sang their own songs
And he who sent to Nature back,
    Some answering notes,
Sing on, but we hear not their song!

The harp in tune to common strains,
The harp that lent chromatic tones,
    Both dumb!
The hands that swept their chords,
    Are still:
The hearts that beat in rhythm true,
    Throb not;
The organ notes are silent now;
The master's requiem, who can sing?

TO "CAROLINA"

THE solemn train passed where we stood,
From Gettsyburg to Hollywood.
The faithful comrades bore their dead,
And loving hearts then freshly bled.

We watched them moving sadly by,
My tearful brother-man and I;
Not clad in gray, nor clad in blue,
But white by light and nightly dew.

By death their courage measured be,
From foe of man they would not flee;
Brave, fronting death from death set free,
When battle echoes shook the sea.

The bones of brothers mingled there,
Mine, thine, the caisson's treasures rare;
For blood is blood and heart is heart,
Not battle's fate can brothers part.

THE SISTINE MADONNA

She stands upon the world,
A mother mild;
As if redemption's flag unfurled,
By her sweet child,
Bespoke eternal victory.

Ah, who could win but she!
Birth throes she bore;
Lowly on bended knee,
Opening life's door,
That glory o'er the earth might shine.

Henceforth shall motherhood
Be woman's joy;
And every child find good,
Without alloy
Dawn from the life of Mary's Son.

Go back to Bethlehem town,
Ye children go;
Surpassing in renown,
All worlds can show,
Behold the City of our Lord.

There, mothers, tread the ground,
The virgin trod;
Who in her new born infant found,
The Son of God,
The joy of holy motherhood.

There, children, echoes wake,
Angels are nigh!
Bethlehem forever make,
Glory on high,
Songs of the maiden mother's child.

ANNIVERSARY ODE

A VERY old legend has told,
How chemists took ashes of flowers,
That rarest Greek vases could hold,
And wove them in wonderful bowers.
But color and fragrance were lost,
The day of their beauty was done;
Fresh flowers after fire and the frost,
Draw perfume and tints from the sun.

The man to his work of to-day,
In pulpit, on platform and field,
Comes forth in no alchemic way,
From mythical vases unsealed.
All his years a target he's stood,
Look how he is battered with shot!
Still heart-pulse and rhythm are good,
While he fronts the fires that are hot.

The champion of all human rights,
Like Nelson at Trafalgar brave;
Great leader of crusading knights,
Not sepulchres but men to save.
Somehow, tho' one may not tell how,
The old steel blade brightens with use;
And hot burns the share of the plow,
That grinds against rocky abuse.

O fearless, and passion filled man!
Cast in the alembic of truth;
Let earth foes fight fierce as they can,
They'll spoil not the dew of thy youth.
Christ's man dwells serene in Christ's light,
The Prince of Peace outgenerals Mars;
He scatters the darkness of night,
His glory outshineth the stars.

THE NEW DRESS

ARTISTIC quite, and rich the dress,
Graceful in style, one must confess;
But most adorned by every grace,
That shines in lovely soulful face.

No silks, nor gems, one half so fine,
Tho' they like pearls of beauty shine;
They equal not her smile when nigh,
Nor flash of her own lustrous eye.

Love loveliest is when unadorned,
Deft artists be forever warned;
Ye cannot hide love from my sight,
Nor shut its sweetness from the light.

THE BURIAL OF DR. SAMUEL F. SMITH

SING low, O children, sing!
Like birds on weary wing,
Flags droop in silence, at half mast,
Sing low, a soul has past.

Past out of crowded town,
Echoing the sweet renown;

Past in to fair Immanuel's land,
Where white robed singers stand.

The anthem of the free,
Your legacy shall be;
Song notes in ecstasy fling down,
And wreathe the autumn crown.

His sun shines on in peace,
Where glories never cease;
The country without gloom of night,
The dwelling place of light.

Sing low, celestials near,
Songs of the earthly hear;
Gently, the holy praises bring,
Sing low, O children, sing.

HOME LIES JUST THERE

IN MEMORY OF GEORGE M. STARBIRD

Not now in measured years,
Can lives we love be told;
Not fleeting hopes, nor transient fears,
Are able loves, or lives, to hold.

This earth exceeding fair,
For souls too narrow lies;
Across its bounds of sea and air,
The spirit to its freedom flies.

Break not then tender hearts,
When love ties seem to fail;
Say, when the loved gently departs,
Home lies just there, within the veil.

The life of love is there,
No fading hopes, nor fears;
No bonds of pain, nor restless care,
Joy there and peace without earth's tears.

AN AFTERTHOUGHT OF MEMORIAL DAY

SWEET flowers bloom every Summer,
Earth's garden freshly gleams
To welcome each fair comer,
Aglow with sunlit beams.

Like some new creature springing
Out from the womb of earth,
See nature pure life bringing
In the holy hour of birth.

Frankincense, myrrh and aloes,
   Pure odors freely shed,
While love dear memory hallows,
   They bloom above the dead.

These are the emblems fragrant
   Of beauty and decay,
Life in night's bosom latent
   Leaps forth with rising day.

Forevermore returning
   As refluent shore-lapped waves,
The mother comes discerning
   In sleep her fallen braves.

She wreathes their tombs with roses,
   Fresh every Summer time,
And while calm death reposes
   Watch angel guards sublime.

Glad resurrection glories
   Where buried heroes lie,
Crown monumental stories
   That kiss the arching sky.

THE RAVEN AND THE FOX

Translated from Lafontaine

MASTER raven, perched upon a tree,
Held in his beak some cheese;
Master fox caught the fragrance with glee,
Drawing near with bland pleas—
How happy, how beautiful now!
If your voice is sweet,
As your plumage is neat,
The phenix of foresters thou.

Master raven, with pride in his eyes,
To lift up his fine voice,
Opened his beak, and let fall the prize;
Then the morsel most choice,
Master fox seized, and blandly said,
My very good sir,
Your cheese I prefer,
Tho' of songsters you are the head.

This know that each flatterer must live,
At the cost of that one,
Who to proud words heed only will give;
With this lesson I'm done—
For very well learned it has been,
'Twill pay for the cheese,
Which my taste will please,
And help me my living to win.

ENVOY
Master raven, ashamed and confused,
Swore he'd not be again so misused.

OUT OF THE TOMB

Out of the Tomb in the early morning,
Out of the dark into beautiful day;
Calmly victorious, glory adorning,
Comes the world's Savior now opening life's
    way.

Escort of angels, joyful descending,
Radiant as lightning, and clad in heaven's
    white,
Move at his bidding, the sealed earth rending,
And filling the tomb with the glad daylight.

Morn of the risen Christ, wondrous dawning!
Shadows of death all bidden to rearward;
Day breaks eternal, sun rays prolonging,
Flash on the footsteps of Jesus our Lord.

Out of the Tomb, and into the glory,
Robed for his crowning, and the great white
    throne!
Bow and adore Him, chanting the story,
Follow, ye ransomed, He calls you His own.

A SONG TO THE LYRE BIRD

From the southland a beautiful bird,
Under the pure azure sky,
Brought sweeter song than ear ever heard,
In sunshine where songbirds fly.

Then there came to my heart a great joy,
At sight of the song-bird near;
And a love with its tender decoy,
Poured songs in the songster's ear.

    O bird of the southland,
    My beautiful bird,
    Hear what my heart sings.

A song to thy luster full eyes,
In praise of thy lyra like wing,
The brightness of southerly skies,
The glory thou didst with thee bring.

Fly, fly, bird of love, to my heart,
There built I for thee thine own nest;
O bird of the southland, thou art,
To find, where thy love is, thy rest.

    O bird of the southland,
    My beautiful bird,
    Hear what my heart sings.

THE LIFE OF LOVE

O HEART of love, my own sweet heart,
I hold thee mine, since mine thou art;
The loving gift thou gavest me,
Thyself in love received of thee,
    A heart of love.

O soul of love, my own sweet soul,
To thee I yield in dear control;
As thou to me thyself doest give,
Thy breath divine shall make me live,
    O soul of love.

O life of love, my own sweet life,
Thy life, my life with beauty rife;
Since thou the life of life to me,
Forevermore thy life shalt be,
    O life of love.

O loving heart, O heart of love,
As star of light in skies above;
Thou shouldst light on all my way,
Thy love the joy of night and day,
    O heart of love.

O loving soul, O soul of love,
In brooding nearness, as the dove;
Thy power of presence changes quite,
All inner strifes to calm delight,
    O soul of love.

O loving life, O life of love,
Eternal in thy heaven above;
Live thou in me, myself in thee,
Thy deathless light my glory be,
    O life of love.

GETHSEMANE

Across the bed of Kedron's brook,
A garden slope bends towards the west;
Whose olive shades give peaceful look,
When day is done, inviting rest.

Gethsemane, devoted place,
Scene of most holy, fervent prayers;
When Christ, with upturned, pleading face,
Laid at God's feet his load of care.

Gethsemane, Gethsemane,
What echoes rang thro' all the air,
When Jesus would from pain be free,
And yet bore all, pressed on him there.

O glorious garden of the Lord,
Where heart by angel touch upborne,
To Father's heart, in sweet accord,
Was bound in love, by grief yet torn.

Gethsemane, whose saddening hour,
Grew sadder still to Christ alone;
When traitor's kiss proved Satan's power,
To drive a soul beyond atone.

Gethsemane, the garden sad,
The tenderest spot beneath the sun;
Since Jesus in deep sorrow clad,
Prayed, "Not my will, but thine be done."

Where art thou, my Gethsemane?
When with my burden and my care,
I, as my Lord, shall strengthened be,
Thy will be done, my answered prayer.

HYMNS OF THE NATIVITY

MAGNIFICAT

My soul doth magnify the Lord,
And in my Savior God rejoice;
For he my low estate hath seen,
And made all peoples call me blest.

Great things the mighty One hath done,
For me and holy is his name;
His mercy is on them that fear,
From age to age, from year to year.

He showed the strength of his right arm,
The proud in heart he scattered far;
Cast down the haughty from their thrones,
Exalted them of low degree.

He filled the hungry with all good,
Empty, the rich he sent away;
He helped his servant Israel,
Mindful of mercy evermore.

BENEDICTUS

Blessed be the Lord our God,
He his people hath redeemed;
And salvation's horn raised up,
For us in his servant's house.

GONE HOME TO GOD

IN MEMORIAM OF DR. ALVAH HOVEY

Gone home to God.
His home on earth was like
The paradise of old,
Where daily he could walk and talk,
'Mid revelation full of grace,
And live with God.

At home with God,
In truth and love and deed,
Nor hid from face divine;
Fearing not the Almighty's voice,
But coming near to hear the word
That came from God.

At home with God.
With brother men at home,
To speak progressive truth,
That unto him was newly told,
Through all the earnest sacred years,
He walked with God.

Gone home to God.
His home in heaven like
All his high hopes contained,
His far, true vision daily scanned;
Welcomed by his best friend and Lord,
Home, home to God.

Gone home to God,
Think not of him elsewhere,
Rest and renewal there;
In the great treasure house of truth,
Thought answering truly thought divine,
O! home with God.

From home of God,
This son of God and brother man,
Sends messages to-day,
And thrills the soul he stirred of old,
To lead men on in ways of life,
Home, home to God.

A GOSPEL SERMON

Ho, Boston wants a new emotion,
Not soothing cordials, nor a lotion;
But some magnetic shock or power,
Some Roentgen flash to light the hour,
Let in the sun-burst's constant ray,
And shine away the dark of day;
Then Henson came, as if from Hermon,
But only preached a gospel sermon.

THE CHRISTMAS KING

Over mountains, over the hills,
And by all the running rills,
Far away from shore of sea,

We leap across the bounding brooks,
Where the song bird has his nooks,
After the glorious Christmas tree.

Among the graceful pines 'tis found;
Where the evergreens abound,
Its lithe pendent branches see.

Tree of trees! so pliant, slender,
Gracefully to us surrender,
And you shall enthroned be.

We will bear thee to thy palace;
And in honor quaff the chalice,
While the maidens garland thee.

When they've wreathed, adorned and crowned
    you,
With festoons twined gaily round you,
Royal-robed king you shall be!

Now to your Majesty we pray,
In your heart may there be no nay,
Hear, as we petition thee.

Gifts of your love grant to us all,
Remembered be the great and small,
'Neath the kingly Christmas tree.

And upward through thy branches light,
Our thankfulness we'll send to-night,
For the Christmas king and thee.

MIDNIGHT

One passing moment, only one,
The old year's done, the new's begun!
Ring out, O bells! around the world,
Where'er the Christian flag's unfurled;
We measure time by Bethlehem's star,
It shines o'er sea and land afar.
It guides the East, leads on the West,
And sheds its light upon the blest!

Stop, thoughtful souls, turn, grateful hearts,
Think as the old year now departs,
What bounties filled the fleeting past,
What mercies shall the years outlast!

For years will come, and years will go,
In gladness some, and some in woe!
But heavenly mercy never ends,
While starry cross above us bends!

Midnight is past, the morning breaks,
From night and death the earth awakes;
Greet brother man with words of grace;
Cheer brother man with hopeful face;
Keep patient heart, who burdens bear,
For goodness helps the load to share,
Requites all losses, checks all tears,
And makes worth living all the years.

Then ring, O bells of heaven, ring!
And bid us with the angels sing.
Glad morning of the New Year's day,
Sheds light and love on all our way.
Ring out the old, ring in the new;
The false shall die, but live the true,
Till years are done, all blessings won,
Bestowed on man by God's own Son.

HEAVEN'S GATE

TENDERLY bearing their spices and balm,
  Came women in loving accord;
Filling with sweetness the resting place calm,
  The tomb of the crucified Lord.

Wondering they saw the tomb open and bright,
 The angelic glory shone there;
But they scarce heeded these visions of light,
 Their hearts were oppressed still with care.

Where have ye laid him, our Lord let us see,
 Our soul's love, O find him we pray;
Heaven on high e'en no heaven would be,
 Our Lord from us taken away.

Tenderly bearing the spices and balm,
 They turned in their saddened accord;
But his own voice filled with heavenly calm,
 The tomb of the crucified Lord.

Needing not spices when Jesus we see,
 His life is our life's sweet accord;
Heaven's gate forever to us it shall be,
 The tomb of our crucified Lord.

ALL, O LORD, IS THINE

NOTHING, Lord, I give by measure,
I am Thine, I call Thee mine;
Thou my soul's one priceless treasure,
Let me say, my all is Thine.

Hold me, Lord, by love's strong fetter,
Fear I naught beneath Thy sway;
Liberty can be no better,
Master, rule me day by day.

All the good, for which I'm living,
Is the good of God to me;
Let me use what He is giving,
Till mine eyes His glory see.

A MOUNTAIN VISION

TO W. H. WELLS

On a mount where the mists of the morning,
Beyond me lay heavy and gray,
The twilight giving place to the dawning,
And clouds lighting up with the day;
I stood, before a Brockenlike specter,
All regal in bearing and mien,
With the crown and the kingliest scepter,
Made brilliant in day's early sheen.
A troop of singers sweet-voiced, sweet-favored,
Filled the air with a glad refrain,
And their song of the olden songs savored,
That echo reëchoes again:

Three score years and ten are ended,
Life's great battles now are won;
Where the bravest hopes extended,
Fall the footsteps 'neath the sun.
Memory tells its grateful story,
Morning sends its light afar,
Tho' the mists of mountain hoary,
Vanish with the earlier star.

On a crest where the mists of the morning,
Long since had all melted away,
And some canopied splendor adorning,
O'er all the far lofty height lay;
I saw not now the mystical specter,
But a soul in manly array;
Beside him, richer than crown and scepter,
Lay trophies in kingly display;
And there gathered affection's grief bringing
Some notes of a happier song,
Than the elder songs plaintively ringing,
Yet helping the new to prolong.

No, not old, for years are coming,
Fresh with deeds of goodness done;
As in spring when birds are humming,
Some old tune anew begun.
Yonder read the unfolding story,
Eyes behold with vision clear,

Off the crest of mountain hoary,
Heavenly foregleams lingering near.

Height of the morning, crest of the noontide,
In shadow-land, specter-land stay!
Down the westering slope, towards the eventide,
Thro' dark and night cometh the day.
Join then the past years with the eternal,
Where blessed immortals attend;
Hastening on, hastening on, sun supernal,
Make life and its good deeds to blend.
Fall benedictions, where ends my vision,
With the birth-song I sing to-day;
Down the slope, on, to sweet fields elysian,
Divine one, O lead thou the way!

A LOVER'S SONG

COME sail with me in my staunch lifeboat,
   On fair tho' untried sea;
There was never a truer ship afloat,
   To brave the stormy lee.
Should I fail to steer by the beacon light,
   I'll track the good hope star,
And drop the anchor safe at night,
   By shore now seen afar.

Come dwell with me in my own dear home,
   I built for thee and thine;
By sea and forest no more we'll roam
   Where rock the wave and pine.
I cannot be now of toil afraid
   With a heart from care set free;
For the toil of my life is all repaid
   When home is filled by thee.

The song of my soul is love's own song,
   I sing it loud and clear;
Its echoes the land and sea prolong
   And she I love doth hear.
Then need no more my voice arise
   To call my love to me,
I listen with sweet and glad surprise
   To answering song from thee.

AN INCIDENT

I TOUCHED the cheek of a little child
Of sunniest face, and eyes so mild,
I could not think it a fancy wild,
It was the cheek of my sainted child.
   She passed me in the way.
   Recalled the dark sad day,
   When in our arms she lay,
   Our dear dead child!

She turned and gave me her sweetest smile,
And in that moment banished all the while,
I've mourned and wished, my soul to beguile,
That sunniest face, that sweetest smile.
   I knew, in that one day,
   Some fair far shining way,
   I'd tread, and then would play
   With the dear child!

I knew her living, and I could wait,
And still my grief, that, early and late,
Had saddened my path towards heaven's gate,—
To see her face I'll patiently wait.
   Wait for the coming day,
   Watch for the shining way,
   Where we our love shall lay
   Beside the child!

INSPIRATION TO MISSION WORK

By the lives of martyred preachers
  On the blood-stained shore;
By the souls of earnest teachers,
  Sainted evermore,

Onward bear the gospel message
  Jesus dying gave.
Faint not, fail not: death's the presage
  Of Christ's power to save.

While they rest by Orient rivers,
  'Neath the rolling wave,
Where swift arrows from death's quivers
  Pierced the hearts Christ gave,

Mark the way o'er all the islands,
  Continents and seas;
Note the steps along earth's highlands
  Trod by such as these.

Spirit from the Father's bosom,
  Rule thou over all;
Make them know the eternal ransom
  Whom the Lord shall call.

VOICI LA CASCADE

In the pictured way towards Chamonne,
Beyond Lake Leman's shore,
Alps rise on Alps galore;
Till mountains into mountains blend,
And far Mont Blanc brave travelers see.

Sometimes the mists becloud the eyes,
And light on darkness lags;
In wooded paths, or crags,
That towering, frowning, threatening death,
Pour laughter down as from the skies.

There high aloft to guard the winding dale,
The snowy water stands,
Like girlish dancing bands,
Or on the edge to fling,
Defiant o'er the crest the bridal veil.

Voici la Cascade! rapt gazers cry;
Winds catch the falling spray,
Make mystic wand their play,
The wood nymphs call, the echoes wake,
To clasp the maid whose nuptial hour is nigh.

Caught up, as if from Alpine heights,
Transformed the quiet brook,
Long hid in shady nook;
New joy to bring to Paradise,
New colors blend in newer lights,
Where lakelets from the brooklets rise!

There children toss the pebbles in,
To see the bubbles shine;
Like seafoam on the brine;

Through bridal veils look loving eyes,
And *Voici la Cascade* they shout,
Who feel the glad surprise.

PRAISE GOD, ALL YE FAITHFUL

PRAISE God, all ye faithful, exultant unite,
And here, the glad story of Christ's love re-
        cite;
Immanuel, Immanuel, the great name prolong,
Help, Lord, while we join in the chorus of song.

We glorify Thee, whose kind angel of love,
Thy messenger came with rich gifts from above;
Like children we grew from the old to the new,
And grateful of heart our past blessings re-
        view.

In thy name, O Savior, our banners we
        raise,
And blazon upon them Thine infinite praise;
By grace Thou has led us, Thy power will not
        fail,
The cross is our ensign, let us still prevail.

O Spirit divine, be Thou with us we pray,
In Zion do Thou the chief corner stone lay;
Let children's own children continue the song,
Immanuel, Immanuel, Thy glory prolong.

TO REV. J. P. ABBOTT

A GOODLY place this pastor found,
And made it his fair camping ground;
Where altar fires for years have burned
And loving hearts sweet gospels learned.
   Ordained to preach,
   And souls to reach;
   To bring good cheer,
   In doctrines clear,
   To bear a light
   Through sorrow's night,
   And by the cross
   Save souls from loss.

Welcome, the greeting word at first,
In song, and prayer, and choral burst;
And, *welcome still*, the watchword true,
To preacher and to people due.
   The pastor's care,
   True love will share;
   His words invite
   To love's delight;
   Here welded hearts,
   Though he departs,
   Will bind and hold
   Through years untold.

Good cheer shall echo o'er the sea,
To him this lovely song shall be,
His lullaby when day is gone,
His matin note at morning's dawn.
     No scenes afar,
     Nor sun, nor star,
     Can e'er outshine
     Past days divine;
     Old friendships live,
     And gladness give,
     Beyond the new
     Of Orient's view.

God speed, along the pilgrim path,
But keep in mind the household hearth,
Where watch-fires shed their rays and burn,
Like beacons beckoning safe return.
     Roam where one will,
     Drink to the fill
     Of sacred founts;
     Or climb the mount
     For visions rare,
     Naught can compare;
     Home friends are best,
     Home loves most blest.

UNDER THE FLAG *

FOR THE FIFTIETH ANNIVERSARY OF THE CLASS OF 1856 WILLIAMS COLLEGE, 1906

UNDER the Flag at Pocomtuck,
Men of Williams and Amherst met;
Far mountain ranges echoed loud,
Their cheers and rousing songs.
As if old Greylock's thunders
Had joined with Holyoke's roar!
Under the skies at Pocomtuck,
Waved the Flag brave Garfield bore.

Under the Flag at Washington,
Men of Williams and Amherst met,
When war clouds filled the sky;
The Flag meant all to patriots,
Who saw in its blue escutcheon,
The heaven of home and freedom,
Under the Flag at Washington
That Garfield bravely bore.

* October 16, 1855, the class of 1856 of Amherst College met the class of 1856 of Williams College, on the occasion of naming a high ridge, in the town of Charlemont, Mount Pocomtuck. James Abram Garfield, afterwards President Garfield, carried the United States Flag and led his class up the mountain.

Under the Flag at Elberon,
Where the martyred Garfield lay,
Men of Williams and Amherst wept,
For their comrade fallen, dead!
But to-day, strike hands together,
Union, country, liberty,
Still evoke our cheers and songs,
Under the Flag brave Garfield bore.

QUE DIT-ELLE LA FLEURETTE?

WHAT saith the tiny fragrant flower,
To butterfly on joyous wing,
When flitting gayly o'er her bower,
In lowland cool, by mossy spring?
Go not away, rest here with me,
If I am sweet, it is for thee.

I ask thee now to come to me,
Alight, and stay close by my side,
From earthly chains I am not free,
While thou thro' heaven dost freely glide;
Go not away, rest here with me,
If I am sweet, it is for thee.

O fleeting one, whom I adore,
Take pity on my low estate;
The captive who doth thee implore,
Will she survive to-morrow's fate?
Go not away, rest here with me,
If I am sweet, it is for thee.

LOVE'S LABOR LOST

TO E. F. B.

It cannot be
    Love's labor lost!
Heart, hope and soul.
    Whate'er the cost
Declare the truth,
    It cannot be.

It has not been,
    Since holy will,
Determined all,
    Love should fulfill;
All worlds and hearts,
    Combine to tell,
That holy will
    Does all things well.

As God works on,
    In wondrous grace,

The radiance of
    His loving face,
Shines clear and far,
    In darkest night;
Nor leaves one spot,
    Enshrouded quite;
For love loves on
    In sweet content,
When love in love,
    Best days are spent!

Love toils in hope,
    And knows no cross,
Can hide the day,
    Nor fear the loss
That broods o'er life,
    That wastes away!
Since yonder see,
    Beyond the past,
All hope has sought
    Appears at last;
While only this
    Remains to tell,
Love's labor lost——
    No, all is well.

THE BLUE EYED BOY

BRIGHT as the sky of a sunlit morning,
Deep with the blue of the far away day;
Full round eyes the pure home life adorning,
Flashing with sunlight shining care away.

Whence came they bringing charm to this
    household,
Out of what azure deep calling to deep;
Leaped the color tone in beauty untold,
Richer than treasures that fairies would keep?

Long have they sparkled where love's jewels
    shine,
Those eyes were love's gift to this lovely boy;
They were mine, said Love, now they shall be
    thine,
My gift to thy home shall bring endless joy.

Shine on in the light of the lovelit eyes,
Sunbeams and starbeams can bring no alloy;
Love's gift is precious, the unsullied prize,
Edward Lord Harvey, the bright blue eyed boy.

JESU BONE PASTOR

Jesus at thy footstool kneeling,
Hear our humble, fervent prayer;
Naught within our hearts concealing,
Objects of thy tender care.
Let thy blood, the healing fountain,
Fill us with life giving power;
Leave us not on sin's dark mountain,
Keep us in temptation's hour.

O thou great, good shepherd, lead us,
Out of death and into life;
By the placid waters feed us,
'Neath the shadows, far from strife,
There in mercy's arms infolding
Bear us on along thy way,
Strong, thy precious love upholding
Thee to serve, through all life's day.

Ministries on earth are ending,
Still with us Christ's words abide;
Death and life while now contending,
Show the Cross the Crown beside.
O thou shepherd ever gracious,
Blend in love our hearts to thine;
In thy heavenly kingdom spacious,
Blessings give, like thee, divine.

Amen.

EXCURSION RHYMES

AT HOME

COME over the sea to Rhynland,
Said my sister to me one day,
We'll revel with legends and fairies,
And while the summer away.

I'll go o'er the sea to Rhynland,
Like a fairy or a fay;
I'll dance while the wild waves shall bear us
Wherever the wild waves may.

AT SEA

Oh, woe worth the day, to Rhynland,
I promised my sister to go;
Blue waves and sea breezes appall me,
I'm food for the fishes I know.

But were I as bad for digestion,
As Jonah who swallowed the whale,
Like him I would take my direction
For home in a three days' sail.

AT HOME AGAIN

Home again from fairy Rhynland,
There's no place like home to me,
I bow to the streets and the shadows
Of neighbors and friends I see.

Put me in my little bed, mother,
Home rest is the best for each day,
And Cora may go with another
To hear what the wild waves say.

AFTERTHOUGHT

Seas passed and dreams of the Rhynland,
Glad memories to sister and me;
Gone, gone are the waves and the shadows,
Songs only resound o'er the sea.

DREAMS

Dreamed I once in fancy's Castle,
Brooks to flowing rivers run,
And rivers run to sea.
Then fancy growing idlewild,
Ran off to sea with me,—

To Belgen land and Rhynland,
To Switzerland and France,
Old England, Scotia, Ireland,
All in a waking trance.

Turning back to home land Castle,
As the brooks to rivers run,
And rivers run to sea,
Fancy no longer idlewild,
Brought notes for you and me.

SEQUEL

I'd write a book—
Of physics, metaphysics,
Of ethics and æsthetics;
Of mental work and working,
And thought in secret lurking,
I'd write a book.

I'll write a book—
My ideal book discarding,
My soul no thought retarding,
I'll look and read off nature's chart,
And scorn the metaphysic art,
I'll write a book.

I wrote a book—
Of what I plainly saw and read,
Of what my God had done and said
To me, his child, in language grand
In native and foreign land,
I wrote a book.

THE SYRIAN BOY

IN MEMORIAM OF DAVID ABDALLAH

I am sure that Jesus loved him,
  As he looked from heaven above,
When the Christian mother bore him,
  On her mission work of love.

All the years the boy was learning,
  As he trod the lowly land;
Where the rugged ways were turning,
  While he held his mother's hand.

Beside the lake of Galilee,
  He learned the stories told;
At Jacob's well he seemed to see
  Jesus as in days of old.

But voices called to him afar,
  O'er the great and widening sea;
There Syrian bands 'neath freedom's star,
  Found new homes and liberty.

Thither he came and here to find
  What became his Christian shrine;
Vows to God he made and signed,
  "Here, O Lord, my life is thine."

Not many fought on earth as he,
  Though short yet brave the story;
On this far shore of sounding sea,
  He fell and passed to glory.

I see him now from earth toils free,
  Far away from sweeping tide;
Celestial life his boon shall be,
  For he stands at Jesus' side.

HEAVEN'S AMEN

TO MR. W. J. LEACH AND FAMILY

MORNING bells were dumb in steeples,
    Chants of choirs were done;
Homeward turned the reverent peoples,
    Worshiping God's Son.

From an upper chamber winging,
    Passed a soul away,
To the unseen angels singing,
    On that holy day.

Autumn's sun stood in the zenith,
    Earth looked up in peace;
And the symbol told what meaneth
    This home light's surcease.

It was high noon in the highest
    There the glory shone;
In the place where saints stood nighest,
    By the great white throne.

While the earthly house was silent,
    As when day is done;
Light that years the arching sky lent,
    By the darkness won.

Then a child, bright flowers, came bringing,
  Gladdening home again;
And they heard the mother singing,
  Heaven's own sweet Amen.

REUNION ODE

WHERE rivers flow, whose wave on wave
  Meets patient shore in rhythmic beats,
And mountains, o'er whom storm gods rave,
  Look down on life that ne'er retreats,
Beneath fair autumn skies to-day
  Our household bands fresh greetings give;
Heraldic impulse paves the way
  And leads while home loves in us live.

Let epic verse laud with its song
  Our heroes holding sinewy sway,
And tuneful legends glad prolong
  The tributes grateful children pay.
The Conqueror's blood throbs in each vein,
  The ocean's force its vigor sends,
The fertile soil of mead and plain
  New virtues to new heroes lends.
Ancestral lines bind evermore,
  For daring souls girt with fresh might
Their native strength impulsive pour
  On dwellers 'neath celestial light.

Transmitted worth is lofty source
  Of living power, while sunlit arch
Gives echoing bugle notes their force
  And sky tones bid the onward march.
Rise then aloft to spirit heights,
  Our home-bound guide with winged feet
Flies where the upward path invites
  And households in their heaven will meet.

FAITH COTTAGE

Home by the summer sea,
Where light and shade combine;
In storm or calm restful and free,
Here hearts their cares resign.

Fresh breezes lift the waves,
The air of heaven one breathes;
So pure the very soul it saves,
And life to beauty cleaves.

Enlarging glories come,
Faith forms a grander zone;
Hope adds to the ethereal sum,
The cottage holds a throne.

For love encircling all,
Of earth and sky and sea,
Makes of the home a palace hall,
Faith's dwelling place to be.

TO JOHN G. WHITTIER

He caught the note of nature's lays,
He heard and wrote for coming days,
     Their echoing song.

Along the hills, that bloom with flowers,
By murmuring rills, beguiles the hours,
     His echoing song.

His heart rang out for right 'gainst wrong,
Its foes to rout, with freedom's song,
     His victor song.

Poetic soul! Spirits of truth,
At heaven's goal, by founts of youth,
     Echo thy song.

Live in the peace thy pure life brings;
It will not cease, while each child sings,
     Thine echoing song.

THE TEA PARTY'S SECRET

THREE ships came sailing, sailing,
In seventeen seventy three,
From far away East Indies,
And laden down with tea;
For Boston town straight steering,
Their Captains cried, Ho! ho!
There'll be some fine old cheering,
When tea-chests dockward go.

But Philadelphia stockers
Inflamed the Boston Men;
They swore great bouncing swear words,
Each Puritan gave ten,
That no tea-chests should land,
Though old Hutch. prated loudly,
His stern words of command.

Fair Faneuil Hall rocked grandly,
And infant rebels grew;
The cradle of our liberty
Held giants strong and true.
Out rushed the bold young freemen,
And shipmen heard them say:
These ships shall sail off homeward,
Nor in our bay shall stay.

Back, back, ye English sailors,
Or, by our might and main,
We'll sink your black pirate craft,
Or lay some deadly train!
In Mohawk garb rushed madly,
These fifty Yankee men,
Like blood-hounds after tigers,
Their eyes flashed lightnings then!

Oh, how old Boston harbor
They set a-boiling high!
A mighty tea-pot tempest
Curled upward to the sky!
Back, back, the frightened sailors,
To England sailing sent,
While all the smashed up tea-chests
To Jones's locker went.

And now the dames' fair daughters
This teasing story tell,
While Souchong, Hyson, Bohea,
They sip, as each loves well;
But ne'er a woman older,
Nor younger e'en would say
Whose husband, or whose lover,
Turned Mohawk on that day.

PLANT THE STANDARD THERE

PLANT the Standard there—
Where advancing forces gather,
In new lines of circling light;
Where the outlook broader, grander,
Sweeps horizons, day and night.

Where the old in modern costume,
Proves the youthfulness of truth;
Where the march of moving ages,
Tells the truthfulness of youth.

Where the echoes of all changes,
Strike the drums of listening ears;
Where like wingèd heralds meeting,
Men shall learn the deeds of years.

Where the right smites down wrong-doing,
Where are armies brave and true;
That will falter, fainting, never,
Till the world gives man his due.

Fair escutcheon of the city,
Ensign of its noble name;
Herald of its constant progress,
Guide and guardian of its fame,
Plant the Standard there.

THE COOING DOVE

THE cooing dove,
Its note of love,
To listening ear of tender mate,
Reveals the joy and bliss elate,
While nestling, one ecstatic state
Binds cooing dove,
And mate in love.

The gentle tone,
The ringdove's moan,
With its own dear consummate art,
Once found in tune a loving heart,
And since that day will ne'er depart.
The gentle tone,
Of ringdove's moan.

O cooing dove,
With heart of love,
Thy listening mate gives answer true,
To gentle tones that lives renew,
In echoing notes once learned of you.
O cooing dove,
With soul of love.

WARREN SANGER

His name shall head a sacred page,
And highest thoughts of love engage,
For he was long and kindly known
Where goodness had its gracious throne,
In business, manly, honest, true,
With naught to hide from searching view.

There stood a man long by his side,
Whose only wish, when Sanger died,
Was this—that he might be as good,
And stand at last as Sanger stood
Among the blessed ones of earth,
A man of honor and of worth.

Bring wreath of laurel, for the head,
Of veteran fallen, he who led
Children and youth, a noble band,
In Christ's own way, with loving hand;
His eyes, his voice, his daily walk,
Made sermons sweet of all his talk.

Hail memory, that will e'er enshrine,
Him we have loved, with souls divine,
Among the faithful, saintly ranks,
Who worshiped here, and now with thanks,
Still call us from Immanuel's land,
That we with them at length may stand.

THE MYSTERY OF HOME

TO THE HOUSEHOLD OF MRS. N. C. HILLS

What then is life, but mystery,
In which are joy and pain;
All these in untold history,
Sum up the loss and gain.

It is not told on classic page,
Nor writ in battle's lore;
No deeds of men from age to age,
Add to the mystic store.

Life's ministry is mystery,
Outside the one place, home;
More sacred than Consistory,
When God and angels come.

There *Mother* is the priestess' name,
Where altar fires burn;
While God and angels light the flame,
Of love at heaven's return.

For what is heaven but home renewed,
And they translated are,
Who looked long time and glory viewed,
While heaven seemed afar.

Enough of earth to satisfy,
Give back to earth its own;
Hear now her voice *Salvation* cry,
In heaven's grand organ tone.

Near, near, not far Celestial gates;
Till when, last duties done;
The *Mother* in heaven's home awaits,
Her glory now begun.

EASTER MORNING

MORNING of eternal day.
Day of heavenly light!
Now the darkness speeds away,
Speeds the gloom of night;
For the Lord of light and glory,
Heralded in prophet's story,
As once at the Father's side,
Lives, though crucified.

Morning glad with angel's word,
Word of hope and cheer!
Now the song of life is heard,
Stilling cry of fear;

For through earth shall sound the story
Of Christ's victory and glory,
Who o'er death, in deathless strife,
Wins eternal life.

Morning freighted with new joy,
Joy to darkened earth!
Now the peace without alloy,
Tones the voice of mirth;
All the flowerets freshly springing,
All the birds, their new songs singing,
Follow Christ's own victor way,
Making glad his sway.

Morning of the holy day,
Day of sacred light!
Shining ever on the way,
Out of death and night;
All the souls their ransom singing,
From the tomb to life upspringing,
Victors following their Lord,
Sing with one accord.

SONG OF BROTHERHOOD

TO GEORGE E. MERRILL, D.D.

HEARTS join in fellowship of song,
That echoing spaces shall prolong;
Bear on our prayers, O soul of love,
Like gleams of light on heaven-poised dove.

Hail and farewell, but with us still,
Be warmest friendships and good-will;
At home always on unseen heights,
When brothers share kindred delights.

Girt with true might, all sanctified,
Stand to make strong youth at thy side;
Leader of men, one Master leads,
He rules who for us intercedes.

Take thou the heart of brotherhood,
And with it all celestial good;
Then toils, and deeds, and years shall tell,
The great life song, Hail and farewell.

WE BUILD FOR GOD

Written for the Opening of the New Building of
the New Bedford Young Men's Christian Association,
December twelfth, 1891.

We build for God, enthroned on high,
Whose unseen power is ever nigh;
We build for God by whose sure hand,
The worlds were formed, the mountains stand.

We build for man, of lofty birth,
The child of heaven, sovereign of earth;
We build for man, who builds anew,
In Christ's great name and influence true.

Stand to thy praise, and wholly thine,
The house we build, Father divine;
Dwell thou in us redeemed by thee,
From sin's contagion ever free.

Strong faith in God, strong faith in man,
Weld hearts, shape lives to heaven's own plan;
Then weave the cords of brotherhood,
Of all on earth that makes for good.

Let hope of peace, let love of love,
Christ gained, inwrought, come from above;
Lord God of grace, our Savior be,
Who live, and pray, and build for Thee.

THE LEGEND OF GOODY COLE AND ITS SEQUEL

In old witchcraft days, it is said,
Goody Cole frightened many wed;
And young mothers watched babies well,
For some a strange story would tell,
How down the big chimney she flew,
And stole the young child when none knew,
Leaving there an imp in its place
With the soot of the chimney on its face.

So Goody Cole to jail must go,
That every mother wed may know,
To change her baby for an imp
Would make the witch to death soon limp.

A mother cried, "My child she stole,
Go tell the Judge 'twas Goody Cole!"
"To-morrow she shall die," he said:
Hang her until she is thrice dead."

Just then a sunbeam crossed the face
Of baby, and the grime gave place,
To the sweet smile the mother knew;
The imp was gone, her baby true
She folded in her loving arms,
And felt once more the infant's charms.

Haste, haste away, to Salem town,
Dear husband, we'll Judge Sewall crown,
If he will save dear Goody Cole,
Who never my dear baby stole.

The Goodman Dalton rode all night,
Secured release ere morning light!
Then on to Ipswich jail he sped,
Lest Goody Cole should lose her head;
Her chains fell off, she hied away,
And to her cabin fled that day.
Years passed away, at length she died,
No witches came, nor mothers cried.

SEQUEL

Now hear the sequel we must tell,
It is a story known full well,
In Ipswich town where Goody Cole
Lived till she died and no child stole,
A famous school for girls was built
Where minds with polish rare were gilt.
From far and near they came to learn
But never did a witch return;
Yet still the witchery of love
Returned as lightning from above!
Once a sweet girl from Sunderland
Joined the gentle school girl band.
She bore the name our *clansman* bore
Who dwelt hard by the river's shore.

An only daughter, proud and gay,
To Ipswich school did wend her way.
With witchery of love she won
The heart of a New England son,
Years passed; perhaps the story told,
Some traces of the days of old,
Might still disclose; suffice to say,
Bright sunbeams shone along their way,
And children's children live to tell,
How the Sunderland girl became
Their mother and their pride and joy.
No Goody Cole mixed in alloy,
With all the wealth of Ipswich school
Not one was born an imp or fool.

Here ends the tale of love we tell
Of the Sunderland girl whose spell
Of learning and love at Ipswich school
Too strong the lapse of years to cool,
Too hot for river deep to quench
Holds like the grip of tightening wrench;
Holds all of us in fond embrace,
While we defy the witches race;
And find in each love's shining soul
No *fear* of *imp* nor *Goody Cole.*

RULER OF THE EARTH AND SEA

Ruler of the earth and sea,
Now we lift our praise to Thee;
Mountain heights echoed Thy prayer,
Borne aloft on midnight air,
While thy toiling servants still
Waited Thine almighty will.

Surging seas by Thee are stilled,
Fearful souls with faith are filled;
Waves and shores obedient meet,
Reverent each at Jesus' feet!
Christ who made the worlds in might,
Guides us in eternal light.

Multitudes, with one accord,
Rise to honor Thee, O Lord!
Ruler of the earth and sea,
Let our prayers ascend to Thee;
Bid the human tempest cease,
Calm the world with Thine own peace.

Strong in Thee, O Holy one!
Sanctified by grace begun,
Lead us till life's setting ray
Brightens in celestial day;
Earth and sea and hearts are Thine;
Make our worship all divine.

WHEN THE ROSES FADE

WHEN the roses fade,
Say, what then?
In the earth are laid,
Petals deftly made,
Beauty all decayed,
This say then.

When the roses fade,
Tell this then?
Gone the roseate shade,
With its cheering aid,
Naught for toil repaid,
This tell then.

When the roses fade,
This all then?
Heart on hope be staid,
Beauty undecayed,
Roses in earth laid,
Bloom again.

MIT LUST SO WILL ICH SINGEN

TRANSLATION FROM *FELIX MANTZ*

My willing soul is singing,
My heart rests firm in God;
While this vile world is bringing
My life beneath its rod,
My life that has no end.
I'll praise the Christ of heaven,
Who will my soul defend.

WAVES AND SHORE

THE waves were talking with me one day,
In their old sweet winning way;
I listened while on the beach I lay,
Intent on what they would say.

They told how long they had kissed the shore,
Laved with love the rocks all o'er,
Had whispered, and sighed, and moaned the
     more,
Unmoved the hearts they adore.

They had raved, and shrieked in frenzy wild,
Like a spoiled and petted child;
Had danced and rolled and time beguiled,
From motherly arms exiled.

They had grown cold and frigid and rough,
Had dashed against the rigid bluff;
To show they were made of sternest stuff,
Till the cliff would cry of wave, enough.

I listened and heard from answering beach,
Moaning caves did there beseech,
Headlands a lesson of love to teach,
Soothing waves that seaward reach.

They were still as white winged doves are still,
And restfully played at will,
On the bosom that warmed with the thrill,
They know who love's words fulfill.

And the heart of the rocks o'er and o'er,
Neath this outward rage and roar,
Told the love of the waves for seabeat shore,
That sing their song evermore.

HIS DAY

TO MRS. EZRA W. CHAPIN

Near the spot where he lived,
There he died;
All the way he was led
Joy beside.

And the sun in his sky,
Shone o'er him
Till at length came the end,
At Sundown!

Large place he fills to-day,
Where loves last;
For the touch of his hand
Holds us fast;
He is near, not afar.
Still he lives
In the dear ones he loves,
While he gives
Back his own life to us
At day's dawn.

We'll live on then with him,
Where he goes;
In the far realms of life,
Without night,
His fair face, heavenly lit,
Sends its light
On our pathway, not dark;
The day dawn
Not rayless, but cloudless,
Still shines on!

MIZPAH

THE WATCH TOWER

The Lord watch between me and thee when we are absent one from another.—Gen. 31;49.

Long ages since, in Eastern land,
　As told in story and in psalm,
The patriarch led his household band
　To shade of lofty Gilead's palm.

The wily Syrian chieftain came,
　Like sheik of fierce Arabian tribe,
With eye of rage that flashed aflame,
　To seek for plunder or a bribe.

Jehovah watched the unarmed host,
　In midnight vision warned the chief,
Changed rash assault to words at most,
　And brought to frightened hearts relief.

They built the cairn, lit altar-fires,
　Wrote "Mizpah" on the witness-tower;
With songs and tabrets, harps and lyres,
　There sealed affection's parting hour.

Sweet witness-word of love's intent,
　The "Mizpah" Christian hearts will write,
And altars build of souls content
　To trust Jehovah day and night.

The Syrian's benediction theirs,—
   The Lord watch over me and thee;
Where'er they go, may answered prayers
   Keep them from harm, from evil free.

FLOWERS AT CHRISTMAS

SOMEWHERE, every Christmas, flowers are
   blooming,
       And December is like May;
Birds of Paradise their pinions pluming,
       Carol ever some sweet lay.
This the legend old, poets loving tell;
       Joseph's staff within his hand,
Flowered, and on his head heavenly fragrance
   fell,
       When Christ reached the holy land;
Aaron's rod grew green, and once more budded,
       As in priestly days of yore;
Deserts, that for years lay sere, were flooded,
       With the waving bloom they bore;
Vales were hidden 'neath the Sharon roses,
       Gilead's balm blessed all the air,
White the lilies where the maid reposes,
       Scattering beauty everywhere;

Forest, field, and bank, and flowing river,
       In pure robes their homage paid,
Nature, which the Christ came to deliver,
       Its own Lord at once obeyed.

'Tis no legend merely weird and hoary,
       Thus that Christmas flowers bloom;
There's a land untold in mythic story,
       Without blight, or deathly gloom;
To that starlit, sunlit vale of beauty,
       They are journeying day by day,
Whom the Spirit holy leads to duty,
       All along a flowery way.
Some glad morning waking at the Christ call,
       Standing 'neath the bright hued
         trees,
Where answered dreams of flowerland, fair
  land, all,
       Float like fragrant balm unsealed
Unto every loving heart grown younger,
       Shall the legend be revealed.

THE MEN OF LONG AGO

In lyric splendors girt,
Historic deeds shall stand;
When living voice and harp resound,
With glories that to-day redound,
    To men of long ago.

The might of God their strength,
   To break the bigots' bands;
To build for centuries yet to come,
To add immensely to the sum,
   Of human weal and joy.

For conscience's sake brave souls,
   Dared front the Church and State;
Terrific thunders rolled along,
The lightning's flash proved them more strong,
   On rock-ribbed truth to stand.

A nation's battles fought,
   Along the blood-marked lines,
Have won for freedom and for God;
Grand victories 'neath these prophets' rod,
   Who led the foremost charge.

Write in the rock of deeds,
   That fill their niche of space;
Rosetta Stone, King Mesha's tale,
Sealed Scripture truth shall still unveil,
   And match with truth to-day.

For buried ore of years,
   To-day is minted coin;
Beaten and hammered, burnished gold,
The hate, and wrong and might of old,
   But make it brighter shine.

The coin is ours, thank God,
In circulation free;
It passes current everywhere,
The commerce of the world to share,
The freedom of all lands.

Send, send it on, nor fear,
The mint of God will fail;
His strength is in his sovereign word,
Let ages hear what we have heard,
Truth echo round the world.

WILLIAM SCOTT McKENZIE

He was my friend, in Christ's blest ministry,
We met and both searched after gospel truth,
With all the zeal and ardor of our youth;
Then strove to preach truth's gospel, full and
    free.

He was my friend, e'en when I could not see,
All that to his rapt vision seemed most clear,
For clouds that rolled between, and made me
    fear;
He looked beyond to heights where doubtings
    flee.

He is my friend, and will forever be;
The gospel, that he loved, I love it now;
And bind a hymnic wreath about his brow,
While standing 'neath his monumental tree;
He was my friend, the work he did, to me,
Lends inspiration, hope, security.

LASELL VESPERS

Songs of evening, vespers chiming,
Blend in harmonies of peace;
Upward towards the skies are climbing,
Melodies, when earth tones cease.

REFRAIN:

Sun in arching course declining,
Star of coming night appear;
Heaven to thee our souls resigning,
With thy Sun and Star be near.

Islands of the Blessed shining,
Shed sweet rays across the way;
Where fond hopes round toil are twining,
Gladdening each retreating day.

Notes discordant flee with day dreams.
Matin peals reëcho night:
Greeting swift return of ray-beams,
Vespers wait the eastern light.

SONG POEMS

FOR LASELL SEMINARY GRADUATING CLASS, 1896

Sing of the morning sunshine,
Bright with the blush of day;
Reddening the cheek of Undine,
Painting the flowery way.

REFRAIN:

Voices are chiming ever,
Songs in the light above;
Hearts no power can sever,
Tuned to the tones of love.

Sing of the noontide shining,
Flooding the world with sheen;
Youth for no shadow pining,
Bathes in the joy unseen.

Sing of the evening waning,
Echoes that fade away;
Stars of the night remaining,
Herald the coming day.

LASELL ECHOES

GREETING echoes,
Meeting echoes,
From the wood, the field, the way,
Wakened are by some sweet lay;
Airy voices playing,
Love in answers staying,
Greeting echoes,
Meeting echoes.

Meeting echoes,
Greeting echoes,
Night and morn, and sun-clad day,
List to what the whispers say;
Tones of love ne'er straying,
Naught on earth delaying,
Meeting echoes,
Greeting echoes.

Leading echoes,
Pleading echoes,
Out of hearts that long and pray,
For the land where echoes stay;
Love's home journey taking,
Souls are ever waking,
Leading echoes,
Pleading echoes.

A HOUSEHOLD DREAM

BEFORE the days the silver craze,
Set gold-bugs flitting in the rays,
The sun shot down from eastern skies;
When Whigs and Democrats were wise,
Each in their time, and in the place,
Where politics could not efface,
The battle-scars the victors wore,
Of this brave time I dream once more.

Men every whit of sturdy grit,
Turned up the glebe, indulged in wit,
Tilled acres broad, and held the wealth,
No man could gain by sneaking stealth;

Then cities held the country first,
Nor dared defy its bold outburst;
The Yankee owned himself in fee,
Nor bowed to despot o'er the sea.

One home there was, a thousand more
There may have been, this bravely wore
Its crest of power:—the eagle dares
Far heights nor stoops to meaner cares;
When sky-light down its glory flings,
And truth outshines the crown of kings;
Of that fore-home I proudly dream,
As thro' the years its glories gleam.

The grandsire, patriarch in right,
Stood strong, as Hebrew in his might;
Around him sons, themselves now sires,
Lighting at will their altar fires.
We know him well, if he should rise,
His face, his nose, gray searching eyes,
His porte, his mien, his manly way,
Describe our clan, as sure as day.

His wife and grandson, loving, true,
Kept grace, and beauty sweet, in view;
Did ever man, who bore our name,
Find wife, who brought no dower of fame?

Did ever home love's lines efface,
When power thus linked itself with grace?
Of this fair mother still I dream,
Her beauties——now your beauties seem.

I stand again in mansion grand,
As one of this staunch household band;
The parlor is some throne-room fair,
That opens on occasions rare;
Whene'er the parson comes in glee,
On wedding day, or babe to see,
Or somber, solemn, and sedate,
Departed virtues to relate.

The living room invites us all,
The tall clock ticks its welcome call;
With candles, books, and games at night,
The happy folk take real delight;
In chambers, warming pans will hold,
Heat that defies the wintry cold,
And woos to sleep, till morning dawns,
And grandsire raves, while sluggard yawns.

The kitchen, like baronial hall,
Will hold the people, short and tall;
Its chimney take wood by the cord,
Its table feed both child and ward;

By it, when all have paid their vows,
Good toothsome food fills hungry mouths;
And in that kitchen big and bright,
The household gains its grace and might.

The winters and the summers go,
Like seas' and rivers' ceaseless flow;
The men grow, in that homestead, grand,
And women fairest in the land;
They conquer earth, they make the laws,
By all that's human win applause;
School, college, church, best tokens are,
Of home's far light outshining star.

This ancient household is no dream,
By which my dream has worthy theme;
From baron halls, and oaken floors,
Echoes have ceased, mysterious doors,
On shadows gone no more will close,
For they who cast them, find repose,
Where sunbeams ne'er their forms reveal,
While gates of heaven their souls conceal.

But the substance of my dreaming,
Is no baseless fabric now;
Fire lights are from hearth-stones gleaming,
As the stars o'er mountain brow.

Dreams of ancestry fulfilling,
Are the real things to-day;
One, a thousand has made willing,
Proud his genius to obey.

Lives, our lives by might controlling,
In full veins leap forth anew;
And like ocean surges rolling,
Prove us ever firm and true.

Manly powers great victories winning,
Women's aid in smiles and tears;
Hold our ranks, no death shots thinning,
Strong and lovely all the years.

As they passed, so we are passing,
When they had their fill of earth;
We shall stand, as they are massing,
Where God's throne-rays show real worth.

Life, O men, is more than dreaming,
O'er the glories of the past;
Front the future, hilltops gleaming,
Shine with light of home, at last.

Saintly songs along the ages,
Mingle with our songs to-day;
Epics writ on noble pages,
Link life's glories on the way.

Households pass, as dreams are passing,
But they gather into one;
Home bands on the heights are massing,
Home outlasts the stars or sun.

THE LORD'S SEAL

JOIN with angels all ye ransomed,
Seraphs need not sing alone;
God's foundation surely standeth,
For the Lord doth know his own.

Seal of love, divinely fashioned,
Symbol of eternal grace;
Set in crowns of heavenly luster,
Which nought earthly can deface.

Seal of angels, seraphs holy,
Motto borne where sainted go;
Sign of lowly souls in glory,
That the Lord his own doth know.

Lord of life, O God of mercy,
Let thy cross for me atone;
Let me stand among the ransomed,
Whom the Lord knows as his own.

AT THE WINDOW

IN MEMORY OF THE LITTLE SON OF MR. F. L. JACOBS

At the window I saw the dear boy,
All his laughing face sun-lit with joy,
Then I beckoned the sweet child to me:
He answered back in his winsome glee,
 With the light of his eye,
 And the smile of his face,
 With the turn of his head,
 And the movement of grace;
 And I knew there had flown,
 From that window to me,
 The heart of the darling boy.

At the window God saw the dear boy,
His upward turned face heaven-lit with joy,
Then he beckoned the fair child away,
And he answered back in loving way;
 With his pure white soul,
 That knew nothing of sin,
 With the spirit that flew,
 Like a bird on the wing!
 But I wept; there had gone,
 From that window and me,
 The soul of the darling boy.

At the window I see the dear boy,
As an angel's, his face lit with joy,
And the holy child now beckons me,
To his home by the clear crystal sea;
   At the window all bright,
   With its clear heavenly light.
   In the Father's own house,
   In the Savior's kind arms,
   There I see him again,
   And he beckons to me,
   The sainted, the darling boy!

THE STOLEN BRIDE

THE strength of our household is here,
With the skies arched above,
The mountain crests near,
And the air all laden with love;
Where the calm waters flow,
'Neath the summer sun's glow,
And the songs of the birds bring good cheer.

List if you will 'mid scenes so fair,
When hearts swell with pride,
And youth's mad freaks are rare,
To the tale of the stolen bride:

In our Daniel's own time,
And in this goodly clime,
He sought a sweet maid his home to share.

Turning his face one April day,
Off from Sunderland town,
Up stream he took his way,
To Northfield, a place of renown;
Of the maids who lived there,
To him none seemed more fair,
Than Maria Matoon, as they say.

Our Daniel had courted her well,
But the winter was gone,
The flower buds would soon swell,
As love wakes the gay birds at the dawn;
Then married he would be,
And Maria should see,
The new home where as queen she might dwell.

A fine old time wedding they had,
The priest tied the knot strong,
The hot flip was not bad,
And the hours sped with music and song;
Dancers whirled o'er the floor,
While joy reigned there galore,
Till the old folks young again became glad.

But the groom on that bridal night,
Would to his town home ride,
All in the calm starlight,
While the soft couch waited the bride;
"But where is she?" he cried;
"Just now close by my side."
Echo said "where"—with no bride in sight.

Long he waited, then madly roared,
"My stolen bride now restore,
Bring her back," he implored,
And thus thro' the night hours trod the floor;
Then the day dawned at last,
And the agony past,
With the maid to her lover restored.

Who dastardly did the foul deed,
Who stole the sweet girl away,
For envy, or fun, or greed,
The secret is kept to this day;
But happy did they dwell,
And their children's children tell,
How they lived, loved, and died as decreed.

The strength of our homes is still here,
Where the skies arch above,
With the mountain crests near,

And the air is laden with love;
Where the calm waters flow,
'Neath the autumn sun's glow,
And the song of the birds brings good cheer.

GOOD WILL TO MEN

THE morning stars were singing,
The bells of heaven were ringing,
O'er Bethlehem town;
Angels from glory winging,
Their way to earth were bringing,
The Christ child down.

Pure as the lily blooming,
Gentle as ring dove pluming,
In motherhood;
New morning light illuming,
Dispelling all the glooming,
There Mary stood.

Her loving heart with yearning,
The gift of God discerning,
Bent o'er her son;
And from His face upturning,
Light all light earthly spurning,
Upon her shone.

Shepherds their lone watch keeping,
While flocks lay gently sleeping,
    Saw angel bands;
Down shining star-way leaping,
Scat'ring the night of weeping,
    From sorrowing lands.

The morning stars are singing,
The bells of heaven are ringing,
    Sweet now as then;
Since angels their way winging,
To Bethlehem came, bringing
    Good will to men.

MALBONE'S PICTURE

Girt in gold, in colors rare,
Within a jeweled case,
Lies Malbone's picture,
Guarded well;
Its story who can tell?
Three maidens,
Coming, come and gone,
Like twilight, noon and night,
Like bud and bloom and fruit,
A glint of cloud,
A brilliant beam,
A shadow passed away!

He named them each,
This artist fine,
Each his own child,
One *past*, one *present*,
And the *future* one;
Born of his genius,
And of mother time,
Long years they've hung,
On guarded wall,
They ne'er grow old,
They never fade,
These children of the sun.

Come, artist genius, come!
Our past, our Present paint,
Our Future wreath in gold;
Some beams of heaven,
Shadows of earth,
Some coming glories show;
What thou shalt see,
To us reveal,
And guarded well,
With cherished store,
Our inspiration,
And our joy shall be.

Unfold the *past*,
Retreating, vanished, lost?

Ah, no! 'tis glory gone before;
Songs angels sang,
They sing them still!
And tuneful yesterdays,
Mark heavenly lays,
The saints of the past century,
Are singing saints to-day!

Great painter, yet again,
Our *present* tell,
In glowing lines,
In beauty's colors,
Fadeless, faultless, fine, pure;
The eye of love,
The form of grace,
The manly, womanly, the true,
The Christlike, beautiful,
In heaven, on earth,
The same, the century's sun,
Like Son of God, the same!

Once more, O, artist genius, paint,
The *future* paint!
Art has no end,
The times of God abide.
Who, who shall model stand,
For all the morrow's child?

Great God, thy Christ shall be,
Our pattern and our guide;
Make us like pattern rare,
Let glint of heavenly gold,
Crown brows, keep fair,
Christ's loved ones,
Past, present, and to come.

CHARLES HADDON SPURGEON

He lives with God,
The good, the great undying.
Though 'neath the rod,
The shepherdless are crying.

In sad accord,
Hearts bowed with grief are wrestling;
He's with his Lord,
And in his bosom nestling.

He fought the fight,
And now the crown is wearing.
While in earth's night,
Hosts are their armor bearing.

Here, by the tomb,
Share we the endless living;
God through the gloom,
To us His own light giving.

HEAR US, O CHRIST

HEAR us, O Christ! Thou living God,
Thy church, beneath Thy guiding rod,
Would follow Thee, where Thou wilt lead,
Nor hunger know, while Thou dost feed.

Hold Thou Thy cross before our gaze,
By day, by night, in all Thy ways;
Let no earth cloud shut out its light,
No blinding sin obscure our sight.

Thy life our life, Thine open tomb
Our sure retreat from midnight gloom;
We walk with Thee this side the grave,
And feel Thy deathless power to save.

O Risen Christ! O Living Love!
Lead, in Thy light, to light above,
Till all Thy church, for ever more,
Thou life of love, Thy love adore.

ABIDING LOVE

It always was, beginning never,
No time when love could not say I love;
When lovers felt the loveless sever,
Ever love the loving dwelt above.

It always is, in shadow or in light,
Sunshine in the clear or cloudy day;
Everywhere it sheds its radiance bright,
To each lover pointing out the way.

Dear abiding love forever be,
Love abiding leaves no want beside;
Thou my soul's one joy, felicity,
Love, on earth, in heaven with me abide.

TWILIGHT OF MORNING

From isles afar where light is born,
Across the distant sea;
Where orient waves are free,
Whence night and darkness flee;
From fountain, grove and tree,
Come forth the harbingers of morn.

Retreating worlds in upper sky,
Are marching towards the west,
Seeking some place of rest,
Shadows that veiled the crest,
Follow in caverns prest;
Their silence tells the day king nigh.

In robe of brightness, veiled in white,
The stars of early day,
Come on their regal way,
Singing a matin lay,
Chanting what angels say,
Their crowning glories shedding light.

Then faith gives love its fond embrace,
Life pulses blend as one;
Night stars their courses run,
Await the advancing sun,
Night's restful duty done,
And hope and joy meet face to face.

With gentle touch of waking beam,
With breath of balmy air
The glow of nature fair,
The flight of wearying care,
The sweet toned call to prayer,
Hail Easter morn, hail heaven's foregleam.

TWILIGHT OF EVENING

Soft on the waiting hills falls mellow light;
Soft on headland and sea,
As wave on wave moves free,
Fair skies arch peacefully,
Gilding each leaf and tree;
Soft fades the mellow light into deep night.

Song-birds their day notes sung, brood quietly;
The insects' whir is still,
And moving on at will,
Fire-flies the dun air fill;
On marshland, and on hill,
The yellow flash of light but deepens night.

The lingering scenes of sun haste to their
    close;
Nature must have its sway,
Night surely follow day,
The stars hold on their way,
To check each sunlit ray,
And shed their upper light on paths of night.

No will nor art of man can shun repose;
The toiler turns for rest,
Homeward with peaceful breast,
The child by love caressed,
No more with care oppressed,
Forgets the glare of light, to bless the night.

Twilight of evening mild, upon us fall;
When day and work are done,
Battles of lives are won,
Home with retreating sun,
Swift as soft shadows run,
Twilight of evening mild, bring thou each
    child.

MAYFLOWERS

I WONDER whence they came!
Where they slept thro' winter's night,
'Neath what icebergs out of sight;
Who gave to them their name?
These baby flowers of spring,
Sweetest of every new-born thing,
Sweet as songs the song-bird sings,
Or heather bells that ring.

Their fragrance of delight—
Tell to me, its recipe,
Culled from air or sky or sea,
Its magic symbols write;
Then tell the colors fair,
Mingled deftly 'neath the snow,
Painting petals as they grow,
Ah, who has mixed them there?

I think it was the blush,
Tingeing childhood's lovely cheek,
Hard to find, tho' fairies seek,
In evening's gentle hush;
This baby-blush they caught,
And with opening rosebuds hue,
Made the Mayflowers' color true,
Which blush and roses wrought.

One thing sweeter, fairer,
Than these Mayflowers sweet and fair,
Grows as nursed by nature's care,
To be fairer, rarer,
In the world above,
When Arbutus blossoms go
Back again beneath the snow,
Still blooms on—
    The giver's love.

ADESTE FIDELES

O COME all ye faithful, exultant unite,
While veterans surviving, old war tales recite;
Their sons and their daughters harmonious
    prolong,
And children now join in the chorus of song.

America, land of our hope and our pride,
Where peoples and nations securely abide;
O land of the exile, O home of the free,
America ever, the watchword shall be.

For liberty first and in liberty's name,
Let countries afar hear the long, loud ac-
    claim;
These hill-tops shall beacon fair liberty's
    shrine,
Our freemen sheathe swords and in peace still
    combine.

As long as the oceans in rhythmical tide
Roll on and the rock cliffs more strongly abide,
This monument will its own story, full well,
Of country and union and liberty tell.

THE SONG OF THE EXCELLENT WAY

If with tongues of men and angels,
I should speak, and have not love,
Echoing brass, or clanging cymbal,
Tells how vain is all I am;
If I have the gift prophetic,
Mysteries and knowledge know,

If by faith remove e'en mountains,
Naught I am, if wanting love.
Should I give the poor my treasures,
Give my body to the flames,
Without love's abiding presence,
All is profitless to me.

Love is patient, love is kindly,
Envies not, nor boastful is;
Has no arrogance unseemly,
Seeketh never selfish ends.
Self controlled, no evil thinketh,
At injustice feels no joy;
Pure itself, and naught concealing,
Ever joyeth in the truth.
Wrongs love covers with its mantle,
Trusts, and hopes, and all things bears;
Love in loving knows no failure,
Though prophetic powers shall fail.

Gifts shall end their transient service,
Tongues and knowledge pass away;
All imperfect thought and utterance,
Vanish when the perfect comes.
Whilst a child I spake child language,
Infantile my thought and heart;
Now my manly stature gaining,
Childish things I put away.

Now we see as through a mirror,
Heavenly things enigmas are;
When I stand naught intervening,
I shall know as I am known.
Evermore each gracious virtue,
Faith, and hope, and love abides;
But than faith or hope still greater,
Is the all encircling love.

WHEN WHITTIER DIED

"Sweeter than any sung
  My songs that found no tongue."
Whittier.

I THINK the winds, their requiem sung,
In silence rested 'neath the sky;
That waters of pellucid lakes,
Brooklet and river stood becalmed,
  When Whittier died.

In that clear autumn morning hour,
Bird, beast, and dew bejeweled flower,
That joined with him in nature's song,
Yielded to heavenly spirits nigh,
  When Whittier died.

I think the earth was lifted up,
To realms less sordid, where the cup,
The godlike taste poured forth its life,
And holier powers ruled all the day,
    When Whittier died.

New songs with their diviner word,
Were by the listening angels heard;
And he who found on earth "no tongue,"
In holier air began to sing,
    When Whittier died.

BROOK LAWN

PLACE of rest for tired peoples,
Winding ways for children's play;
Arching aisles and leafy steeples,
Worshipful as holy day.

Bloom of springtime, summer's splendor
Autumn's brown, and winter's gray;
Seasons' changes ever render,
Brook Lawn type of nature's sway.

There no city's wild commotion,
Hear I only songs of birds;
Catch the breath of far off ocean,
Feel the music without words.

When I turn with bounding pulse beat,
Wood nymph charming with me goes;
Nearer than I knew the high seat,
Naiads throne of heart repose.

Brook Lawn, telling its sweet story,
Echoing birds and children's lays;
Brook Lawn, scene of brightening glory,
Help to gladden coming days.

OUT OF MY ATTIC WINDOW

Out of my attic window,
Over the roofs below;
While from the heaven light shineth,
Thoughts will swiftly go.

See I through roof and rafter,
Hearts in the homes beneath;
Where in the sun or shadow,
Life keeps constant seethe.

Loftily trees are lifting,
Green branches far in air,
I know tremendous forces,
Send life's pulses there.

Through the great arching skyways,
Fair in the rays of sun;
Or in deep dark of shadows,
There life's courses run.

After things seen, or unseen,
In day, or somber night;
Out from my attic window,
Soul leaps into light.

Far above voice of children,
Winds dreary sough or sigh;
My range and sweep of vision,
Heaven to me is nigh.

Out of my attic window,
To the beloved I know;
O'er roof and tree, and skyway,
Thoughts shall swiftly go.

HAROLD W. HOYT

In pastures green, by waters still,
He loved to roam at his free will;
The sea, the mountain, prairie, plain,
Gave out for him their sweet refrain.

In scenes of day, and gleams of night,
He found some far, and strange delight;
Rare pictured visions passed in view,
For him the world oft shone anew.

Alternate glad and somber days,
Bright flowers beside despondent ways,
Stern battles fought on fields serene,
Proved depth of soul to sight unseen.

His own brave heart, on good intent,
To home and friends rich blessing lent;
Center and soul of love and peace,
Dear memory knows no dark surcease.

For all who loved him, love him will,
While clouds hang low, and spaces fill,
Between this lonely, tearful place,
And that fair light around his face.

The bonds that held him, hold him yet,
While earth and heaven are gently met;
The home he left he gained at last,
Where hope's good bark is anchored fast.

In pastures green, by waters still,
He roams to-day at his sweet will;
The sea, the mountain, prairie, plain,
Gives out for him their glad refrain.

IN A SEASIDE STUDIO

TO MR. WALTER RICKETSON, Sculptor

THE studio built on rocky cliff,
Like eagle's eyrie seemed;
Around it swept sea breezes stiff,
Above it sunbeams gleamed.

But rarer light within illumed,
Unknown to sun and star;
It outshone shield of knight well plumed,
And sent its radiance far.

Beneath its rays fine genius saw,
Creations deftly made;
Rare forms that follow beauty's law,
In sculptured garb arrayed.

Ah, look, the Master bids them rise,
And grandly they appear;
Come, greet them, in the glad surprise,
Of comrades once more near.

The speaking likeness of Thoreau,
Miss Alcott's winning face;
The singers, poets, authors, grow,
Benignant in their grace.

One hour with them, henceforth they live,
With me immortal lives;
The sculptor's touch will to them give,
Glory, that death, survives.

The seaside studio, charmèd place,
Where flute notes echo still;
Where light reveals the poet's face,
When Master spirits will.

Work on, bold sculptor, in the light,
That makes thy studio shine;
Bring back, and hold in living sight,
The forms we hold divine.

OUR HERO

THORWALSDEN, with rare sculptor's art,
In speaking marble's counterpart,
The apostle Thomas reared in might,
Within Cathedral's mellow light.

By mystic art, in wondrous grace,
Of lines ancestral in each face,
Our Thomas, with his lasting fame,
Lives in us all who bear his name.

Behold him, peer of honored men,
When each was brave, with strength of ten;
Whose glory ages shall prolong,
And be the theme of lyric song.

Ho, men of long ago!
In regal splendor girt,
Defying pain, and hurt,
While living voice and harp shall sound,
And blood in throbbing pulses bound,
Let sons your valor know.

Ye saw your day and hour,
To break the tyrant's band,
Subdue an untried land;

To build for centuries coming yet,
While suns cease not to rise and set,
The might of God your power.

For human rights made bold,
Ye faced inveterate foes,
Led on, where freedom goes,
War thunders roll, like seas, along,
The lightning's flash show men more strong,
'Neath duty's flag enrolled.

Your treasures are our gain,
Good hunters of your time,
Authors of wraths sublime;
It passes current everywhere,
The commerce of the world to share,
And human weal maintain.

We send it on, nor fear,
That good of God will fail;
Brave men, whom centuries hail,
We see, and know your sovereign worth,
Great service tells o'er all the earth,
Its echoes comrades cheer.

Then, members of this household band,
Like pilgrims come to fatherland,
Whose shores the limpid water laves,
Bow at the shrine of Thomas Graves.

His goodly heritage is ours;
Led by benignant heavenly powers,
He crossed the sea, midst storm and calm,
A new home won by sturdy arm.

The savage lurked by rock and tree,
He conquered foes he could not see;
He caused the marshland and the field,
Their hidden fruitage to him yield.

Lithe willows marked the winding course,
Of river from its highland source;
In summer glassy, lustrous, mild,
In winter quiet as a child.

THE BATTLE OF THE RIVER

Great river, when the springtide sun,
Made every rivulet seaward run;
When Titan-like, this giant rose,
To play the victor with its foes.

It piled the icebound barriers high,
As if to mingle sea and sky;
It smashed the bridge, the boat, the wire,
Snapped roots of trees like strings of lyre.

It covered islands, leaped the shores,
Swept meadows o'er like dancing floors;
Immersed in its baptism grand
The acres of the newborn land.

The cliffs and mountains stood serene,
Unmoved, it seemed, at this mad scene;
But at their feet the waters rage,
Tore off their mask, revealed their age.

The bed-rock held its fossils well,
Yet surging billows made it tell,
When it embraced the living forms,
Heedless of sunshine and of storms.

Tho' sand-stone hills looked off to sea,
Of Scotia's hills kin claimed to be,
Yet at their base swift whirlpools met,
To grind as millstones newly set.

Old mountains, strong and calm, defied,
The river's scourge that lashed their side;
Endured its mighty rush and sweep
Then rocked it, in its bed, to sleep.

Boast, well they may, these ranges high,
That knows no fear of earth or sky;
Darkness and cloud gird them at night,
Suns, moons, and stars crown them with
     light.

But this bold river holds its sway,
Takes mountain tribute, day by day;
Their Cæsar, they must bow to him,
As castled knights to chieftain grim.

For all this water's summer rest,
Or winter's quiet, coldly prest,
Within the rugged icy banks,
An army is with broken ranks.

Some day at bugle's rallying note,
The army, that the mountains smote,
The embattled victor brings its store,
To enrich the meadows by its shore.

But generous heights need no appeal,
Mount Tom and Holyoke, fired with zeal,
Of their rich treasure freely yield,
To load with harvests mead and field.

Thus battles in the valley end,
In truce, to man, the spoils extend;
Skies, storms, and waters, earth and air,
Bless this good land, this landscape fair.

Our hero stood not here alone,
Proud of this wealth of color-tone;
Strong sons, anew, his right arm nerved,
And daughters loved him, whom they served.

The patriarch led the chosen way,
His tenting ground we tread to-day;
Where'er our home, in east or west,
This spot of earth, for us the best.

Dwellers by sea, on prairie wide,
Or southland stand here, side by side;
Our ancestry and heritage,
Rich now, and on historic page.

Ancestral pride becomes us well,
Heroes, heroic hearts will swell;
All braver we, for brave deeds done,
All conquering still, for victories won.

For blood is blood, that swells in veins,
Which opened leave no coward stains;
The men who bear our household name,
Untarnished keep its lustrous fame.

Our engineers have cities planned,
Our admirals warships proudly manned;
Art, science, poetry, and speech,
Our scholars used, the world to teach.

Our clansmen tracked the savage path,
Unconquered, e'en, by savage wrath;
In revolution's mighty sweep,
From tyranny took freedom's leap.

We tread the way our fathers trod,
Our hero's God is our God;
What name, or sign, or creed, we hold,
His heaven is our eternal fold.

O clansmen bold! O women true!
Honor the man and wife anew,
Whose name, like olive tree and flower,
Lives on in sweetness, beauty, power.

Fall into line, keep time, and tread,
By centuries' columns we are led;
The unseen legions round us bring,
The music of the song we sing.

SONG OF THE UNSEEN LEGIONS

Hark to the tread of forces grand,
As sound of surging sea;
It echoes thro' our fatherland,
In hymns of peoples free.

It knows no halt, and no retreat,
Thro' sweep of circling years;
The banner bright, old comrades bore,
Death shots hurt nevermore.

Great hosts, tho' hid to mortal eye,
Keep guard above our fields;
The foes that fled before us fly,
Blind in the flash of shields.

Hail, hail, brave souls, in music sweet,
As surge of sounding sea;
Ye tread the ways, where chieftains greet,
And chant songs of the free.

O myriad bands, from households dear,
Where laurels crown the day;
Still lead us on, your courage cheer,
Your glory light our way.

AT THE COURT OF HEAVEN

TO THE MEMORY OF A. J. GORDON, D.D.

THIS day let glory's gates unfold,
And praying souls sweet converse hold,
By faith with saints on high;
O listen, and hear seraphic throngs,
Before their Lord sing holy songs,
For heaven to earth is nigh.

Among the blessed see him now,
With shining aureole round his brow,
Whom we commemorate;
Hear his loved word, "I'm satisfied,"
Beholding him who for us died
Arrayed in wondrous state.

This prayer he breathes, on bended knee,
Now from the world of sin set free,
Lord, look in love on me;
Thy will is mine, my glory thine,
My ransomed powers anew combine
And consecrate to thee.

What service here for me most meet,
Where messengers by grace made fleet,
Thy throne-lit ranges sweep;
Among them let me learn to go,
And still thy saving mercy show,
While harvest toilers reap.

The eye of Jesus on him fell,
That look enough his love to tell,
Go, with my joy elate;
Take part in conquests waging yet,
Speed, armed with love, and ne'er forget
The world I new create.

That moment all Mount Zion rang,
With music myriad voices sang,
For joyful tidings came,
Of souls redeemed in far off lands,
Through ministries of gospel bands,
Sent forth in Jesus' name.

New victories all angels cried,
New honors for the crucified,
New crowns about his brow!
Lo, conquering hosts move on their way,
Obedient to his peaceful sway
And all adoring bow.

The Spirit's mission soon complete
Will tell, when all the blood-washed meet,
Cleansed of sin's taint and stain,
Where prayer and praise forever blend,
As through God's universe extend,
The triumphs of his reign.

Swiftly the years, the rays of dawn,
Foregleams of the millennial Morn,
Now leap from shore to shore;
Short grows the promise-lighted night,
Clearer prophetic signs of light,
When death shall rule no more.

Then join your prayers with prayers above,
March on, keep step, in deeds of love,
With those about the throne;
The thousand years to earth belong,
No measure bounds redemption's song,
Where Christ dwells with his own.

Abide in him, O heaven-bound saints,
Above all doubts, and low complaints,
Sing, labor on, and pray;
Wait till the last dark shadows flee,
There at his Court, in glory, see
Christ's Coronation day.

HEAR THOU, MY PRAYER

ALL seeing, gracious Lord,
My heart before thee lies;
All sin of thought and life abhorred,
My soul to thee would rise.

CHORUS:

Hear thou my prayer, O God,
Unite my heart to thee;
Beneath thy love, beneath thy rod,
From sin deliver me.

Thou knowest all my need,
My inmost thought dost see;
Ah, Lord! from all allurements freed,
Like thee transformed I'd be.

Thou holy, blessed One,
To me, I pray, draw near;
My spirit fill, O heavenly Son,
With loving, godly fear.

Bind thou my life to thine,
To me thy life is given,
While I my all to thee resign,
Thou art my all in heaven.

NEW YEAR'S HYMN

Ring out the grateful chime
That marks departing time;
   Its mercies sing.
Cease, tongue of sullen sound,
Life's discords to resound:
Harmonious notes profound,
   Glad anthems bring.

The nation century-crowned,
Whose homes of peace abound,
    Joins in the song.
Where swells the patriot's pride,
Where hearts in truth confide,
While land and home abide,
    The praise prolong.

Blessing beyond the years,
Surviving all the tears,
    Shed o'er the dead,
Answer our faith in love,
Bearing our souls above,
Led by the heavenly dove,
    To Christ the head.

To thee, O Lord, anew,
Love's pledges we renew,
    In sweet acclaim.
Thou, who our Father art,
Keep us from sin apart,
Make us like thee in heart,
    Through Jesus' name.

Our answered prayers are seen,
Like rays of lofty sheen,
    Round heaven's throne.
Hope makes divinely bright,

The new-year's morning light;
We stand in God's dear sight,
Among his own.

LIFE'S BENEDICTION

IN MEMORY OF MRS. CAROLINE M. TRAIN

MAY the grace of God the Father,
With the Savior's boundless love,
When the heavenly spirits gather,
Fall upon us from above.

One more the sainted standing,
Radiant with celestial light;
Where the glory is expanding,
Where her day will know no night.

Not a day on earth too many,
All life's willing work well done;
Never of her mission weary
Till Christ's victories are won.

For o'er land and sea are falling,
Benedictions on her life;
New devotion still is calling,
To the ever blessed strife.

Upward where heaven's blessings blend
May our prayers united be;
And as earth's glories far extend,
Sainted faces we shall see.

THE LURLEI

TRANSLATED FROM H. HEINE

I KNOW not why I am thus saddened,
At legends of old times;
They oft, by day, my heart have gladdened,
While roaming in far climes.

Fancy is free when dark is reigning,
And calmly flows the Rhine;
While shadows o'er the hilltop gaining,
Show daylight's soft decline.

A maiden bright and fair seems sitting,
Upon a far height there;
Rich jewels shine, her form befitting,
She combs her golden hair.

Round glittering comb her tresses twining,
She sings meanwhile a song;
A melody for day's declining,
Whose weird notes echo long.

A fisher in his boat upspringing,
Uttered a wild heart cry;
Forgot the rocks, for siren singing,
With look intent on high.

I saw in thought the waves destroying,
The fisherman and boat;
And knew the maiden's song decoying
Was Lurlei's deadly note.

THE INNER CHAMBER

PEACE dwelt with her, and faith, and gentleness,
And all things else that dwell with souls benign.
Hath she not left these in some visible shrine
Whereunto we may press
In holy pilgrimages, to renew
Our strength that had been weakness but for
    her?
Nay, there is naught for outward view;
I may not open any door and say,
"Here with these trappings of her mortal day
Some living part of her is still astir."

This may not be, but reared within my heart
A secret, inner chamber stands apart,
All furnished forth with her.   There charity
And justice side by side appear,
Not as mere dreams of good,
But as they stood
Embodied in herself unchangeably:
A charity that spreads like shafts of light,
Glowing with warmth and radiance near,
Yet searching, reaching every lair of night;
A justice, like God's mercy, fain to see
In every soul an equal weight and worth,
And, seeing, to withhold from none on earth
The bread of love, the cup of sympathy.
And here, the more to glorify the place
With what she was,
Are ancient firm beliefs in the old cause
Of truth eternal, and, through heaven-sent
      grace,
A smiling courage still by them to live.
Here, too, is humor, warm and sensitive,
Playing like a summer breeze
Through open windows flooded with the sun,
Tempering the air with all felicities
Of true proportion.
Hither I come for solace from the moil
And emptiness without;
And all about

The signs of her—these are so many more!—
Blend as they blent of yore
In aspirations deep
And yearnings oft untold
For them her heart would ever keep
Inviolate from hurt or soil.

These thoughts of her like tapestries enfold
My inner chamber, whence I turn again,
Refreshed, renewed, to face the world of men.

MOSES' ROD

In Moses' hand a shepherd's crook,
  A staff for help on weary way;
In desert paths, by mountain brook,
  To rescue sheep or lamb astray.

The shepherd's crook the rod of God,
  Sign of the Almighty's power and grace;
God's servant bears the mystic rod,
  And meets the Pharaoh face to face.

Then regal power falls by its might,
  Its hidden strength o'erwhelms the foes;
Magicians baffled take their flight,
  And Israel from its bondage goes.

The sea obeys the power divine,
  The uplifted wand rolls back the waves;
The rocks their secret springs resign,
  The rod of God God's people saves.

Symbol of faith and duty done,
  The seal of all prevailing love;
Of dangers past, of victories won,
  Its place all earthly signs above.

Hold thou the rod of God, O man!
  In might of trust redeem thy time;
Thou shalt fulfill Jehovah's plan,
  With heroes stand on mount sublime.

FREDERICK DOUGLASS

LIKE forest oak across whose sweep
The fires of hell have surged in vain;
He stood, where awful lightnings leap,
Undazed, the sport of deadly rain.
The blood within him mingled well,
To grow the giant for the fray;
Philistine hosts could not foretell,
His glory grand in their dismay.

With mighty hand God led him out,
The pillared cloud of fire his guide;
Barbarian forces put to rout,
By heaven's battalions at his side.
Then, after battles, peace sublime,
The crown, and glory of this man;
His name, to read it, higher climb,
It gleams aloft, reach it, who can!

For he was man, man's noble peer,
To honor still an honored name;
The Douglass finding refuge here,
The Douglass winning world wide fame.
Advancing millions, chainless, free,
Joined in the eternal brotherhood,
Standing heroic souls to see,
Behold him lead, who leader stood.

No eulogy in word or rhyme,
Can add to glories bravely won;
Unshackled men, in every clime,
Proclaim his work on earth *well done*.
Keep time then, marching on to-day
To music sung by victor brave;
'Neath bannered freedom's endless sway,
March, country, and the world to save.

THE MISSION HOME

TO REV. S. B. AND MRS. LIZZIE C. PARTRIDGE,
SWATOW, CHINA

By the beautiful bay of the China Sea,
On the rocky highland shore,
That invitingly looks towards the lowland lea,
In sound of the ocean's roar,
    Behold the Mission home.

The delicate touch of the deft Christian hand,
Hath wrought this Eden-fair bloom;
Transformed by its magic the specterlike land,
And scattered the cheerless gloom,
    Far from the Mission home.

Through arch of banyan, pine, bamboo there
    go,
As down old Cathedral aisles,
Those prayer and song voices whose pure,
    ceaseless flow,
Echoes down the deep defiles,
    Around the Mission home.

On the shadowy paths, by the idol ways,
Dark in superstition's night,
Shines now morning's twilight, and the dimless
    rays,
Make the face of toilers bright,
    Within the Mission home.

Up the beautiful bay, and afar inland,
O'er the Middle Kingdom vast,
Hope bids the glad eye see the gathering band,
Multitudes Christ-led at last,
    Come to the Mission home.

From Eagle Rock look, towards the opening
    way,
Through clouds, the mountain tops peer,
The sunsets await the sunrise of new day,
To shine o'er the Empire clear,
    As o'er the Mission home.

POEMS READ AT ANNIVERSARIES OF THE CLASS OF 1856, AMHERST COLLEGE

A CLASS SONG
Twenty-fifth Anniversary, 1881

THE century's quadrant turns to-day,
Its broader sweep of light,
High noon lets down a golden ray,
Life's track is doubly bright.

With faces bronzed by burning beams,
On heights gained by true men,
We stand, recalling College scenes,
And front ourselves again.

The echo of our youthful cheers,
We wake with manly powers;
We feel the heart-beat of the years,
Their matchless glory ours.

As when the mount, in days bygone,
We trod, to nature true;
And crowned Pocomptuck with the song,
We gladly now renew.

All hail to every stalwart son,
Hail, hail each honored name;
Who fallen from the ranks has won
The victor's deathless fame.

The kingliest seat his rightful claim,
Who justly wins the crown;
Their well-earned praise we will proclaim,
And sing to their renown.

Along the way great deeds have run,
And, stepping to their tread,
The gleam of their resplendent sun,
Falls grateful on our head.

We've drunk at many a fount of love,
Of learning had our fill;
We've swept, in thought, an ocean o'er,
Where sail the thinkers still.

The rugged waves, the wintry days,
We braved them as they passed;
No plaint our hearts undaunted raise,
Made tough by every blast.

The harbor line, as sure as life,
Is yonder on our lee;
Like good ships free from storm and strife,
We'll rest in placid sea.

Salute our years, they proudly rise,
Aloft, where centuries live;
Old Chronos had no richer prize,
No costlier boon to give.

But look beyond, not distant far,
Convergent lines will meet;
In brighter path, past sun and star,
Tread now some willing feet.

Foretastes of grander years to come,
Sweet memories here prolong;
Felicity's eternal sum,
The blessing of our song.

CLASS MEETING

Thirty-fifth Anniversary, 1891

"I would like to come back to earth once in a hundred years to see what progress the world has made in the way of truth."—*Goethe.*

Too long to wait, too late to come,
If one must stand on earth to know
The world's advance, as centuries go,
Though German Seer count the sum.

No vision's lost, no sight unseen,
By earnest men in ghostly clime;
They look o'er faith's far heights sublime,
Interpreting the poet's dream.

Fresh laurels crown the Homeric brow,
True science its new tales rehearse,
The classic tongue still sings its verse,
The men who taught us teach us now.

No light of earth the explorer's need,
To note the advance by science made,
He knows the track his genius laid,
Where truth leaps forth with Titan speed.

In touch with Mechanique Celeste,
The old machine he will not use,
For parallax, or sound, or hues;
Beyond the stars he measures best.

The preacher wants no facile pen,
To write the fine scholastic thought,
Heaven's light illumes the word he taught,
Who walks and talks with saintly men.

Our Mather, would he might be here,
To tell with golden speech, once more,
Of Alma Mater, as of yore;
But memory's dear, and heaven is near.

Then, turn not back to search for truth,
While worlds, and centuries forward march,
Stand 'neath its grand triumphal arch,
Beside the fount of endless youth.

OUR DAY

Fortieth Anniversary, 1896

FORTY years, in life's worn time-book,
Mark our day, from sun to sun;
Afterlook illumes the forelook,
Dreams are deeds of valor done.

Cartoons Raphaelesque in sketching,
Hangings see in palace halls;
Gold and silken strands are stretching,
Round stout towers, and frescoed walls.

Back once more, with manhood's treasure,
Where we stood 'neath youth's fair sign;
Homage pay in grateful measure,
At the foot of learning's shrine.

Circling hills where sunbeams quiver,
Call, as bridegroom to his bride;
Meadows, laved by winding river,
Woo, like maiden to her side.

Forests gleam with leafy luster,
Matchless wreath of flowers bloom;
Clouds star-lighted grandly cluster,
Shade and light blend without gloom.

Here the day had hopeful morning,
Where the earth and sky unite;
Man with man, in this glad dawning,
Shared its peace with soul delight.

But war clouds hung with thunder prest,
Above Crimea's mountain crest;
Where allies met the Russian's scoff,
And stormed the tower of Malakoff.

Soon nearer, braver, waged the fight,
Of serried forces for the right;
Battalions strong, whose ranks we trod,
Bore Union banners, bold for God.

War wages still, 'neath noonday sun,
Our battles here are yet undone;
Nor pale we when brave comrades fall,
But front the foe at duty's call.

Brothers, what if noon is passing,
Faces bronzed turn towards the west;
Tinted clouds of light are massing,
Lit by Islands of the Blest.

Back again with lessened number,
'Mid fair scenes, that know no loss;
One by one, in silence slumber,
True men by their well borne cross.

Man by man beyond the ending,
Of this lingering day on earth;
Pass we into fields extending,
Where great souls have deathless birth.

Day of fadeless glory dawning,
Waits us, comrades, by and by;
Part we here, to say—good morning,
Just beyond where shadows lie.

Our day, foregleam of the eternal,
Gathers light from night's decline,
Conquests won, and crowns supernal,
Link brave lives to life divine.

PALINGENESIA

Forty-fifth Anniversary, 1901

Moriturus, who has said it,
Not the God of life and light;
Morituri, we have read it,
Heroes shout it, while they fight.

But from upper regions coming,
Echoes rolled on echoes fall;
Victors victories now summing,
Rouse us, comrades, at their call.

Palingenesia,—hear it!
Men, who seem about to die;
Morituri—never fear it,
We are young, though ages fly.

Hark, rejuvenescent, singing,
Dulls discordant notes of earth;
Listful stand while bells are ringing
Chiming every man's new birth.

Backward never moves our column,
No retractile steps we take;
Forward, steady, slow and solemn,
Strong in ranks that cannot break.

Keep abreast of time's unfolding,
Yesterday is not to-day:
Tents give place, and temples molding,
Merge in temples far away.

Here defy the fires infernal,
Lava blocks no human tomb;
Angels girt with might eternal,
Guard great nature's opening womb.

Souls transfigured, heavenward tending,
Proteus may homeward lead;
Over seas, whose waves descending,
Bear them on with hastening speed.

No Antæus, earth sods treading,
Holds us in his dusty way;
Airy legions wings are spreading,
Gilt, and dipped in sun-lit ray.

Thus keep pace with centuries merging,
Into æons evermore;
Men immortal charging, surging,
Grander worlds will still explore.

Morituri salutamus,
All the deathly let it die;
Namque per fid ambulamus,
Our triumphant battle cry.

KAI GAR

Fiftieth Anniversary, 1906

I SOUGHT for the buried Kai gar one day,
Many dead around, other tomb stones said;
But more were the living that stirred the air,
Tho' no word in stone told their joy or care.
Birds came bringing songs from the southland
    home,
There were flowers and shrubs, green fields by
    the way,
Trees telling their names, where the shadows
    lay,
By the leaves the sun artist penciled there;
Sturdy oaks stood near some hundred years
    old,
They held their stories, the tales of strange
    folk,
Who hunted and haunted the days gone by,
Whose almanac record could not be told.

   Kai gar, an epithet frequently applied to Professor
Nathan Welby Fiske, professor of Greek in Amherst
College, 1824–1847. He died in Jerusalem, May 27, 1847,
and was buried in that city. Professor Horatio B.
Hackett some years later sought out Professor Fiske's
place of burial and caused two cypress trees to be
planted over the grave.
   Professor Fiske edited and translated Eschenburg's
Manual of Classical Literature, which volume passed
through four editions.

Death and life struggled in mightiest grip,
Green blades and monuments blackened with
    age,
Life against death there, and death against
    life;
Which wins, who can tell in the bitter strife?
The living fighting as with giants dead,
Loveliness blooming, arid wastes perfumed,
Tuneful voices silenced the dismal dirge.
I knew them living, brave names they still bear,
None braver, none better to-day than they;
Their souls are alive with our living souls,
Their blood pulses in our own heart felt throbs,
Kai gar is not dead, in fresh forms he lives.
New powers in new beauties ever arise,
Tone anthems of masters antique are heard,
Old swords now welded in strong hands abound;
The soughs of life's battles in forests resound,
Echoing the surge of the loud sounding sea,
Bear them on, ye go, O men in the way,
Though here, yet among celestials we move;
Who can measure soul life by fleeting years?
I shall not die, nor you, not one of you.
We dwell where men will forever abide,
We walk in the light of glory beyond;
It is always our day, shining or gray,
All left undone, worth the doing, we'll do,
Eternity is enwrapping each soul.

Say not yesterday's voices are dying,
Classic myths are but antiquity's lore,
Vanishing visions, echoes of past rimes,
Who cares to remember the olden times?
They say Abt Volger his music forgot,
If a song still lingered within his soul,
Scarcely could his own ear the song recall.
No Homer repeats hexameter lines,
Virgel's pastorals long since were done;
Broken stranded lyres lie strident or dumb,
Beethoven's harpsichord strikes dullards mute,
The song age and singers are passed away.
"Solvitur ambulando" hear, O hear.
This is the world now far away calling,
Babylonia, Egypt and Greece arise,
And give back light from their ambient skies;
Jerusalem casts off its broken chains,
Its morning rays gleam, gone spectres and
        dreams;
A new Rome comes forth from old buried
        Rome,
Nations fight hard to die, yet still they live;
Victims return victors still bearing shields,
Dead epics of poets spring up anew;
The living keep guard at fresh open tombs.
Rouse deathless men, bear your life on with you,
Humanity knows no death nor retreat.
Hear is our Milestone, Alma Mater's sons.

Once far up the mountain dimly it gleamed,
Down mountain sides it will never recede,
Our goal and glory are surely decreed.
We have won it, the battle consummate,
Henceforth we need to make no concession,
While the world full of immortals remains.
Etiam profecto, vanished the shadows,
Dark of the west yields to light in the east,
Manhood and life lose not their power nor
        worth;
We will answer at the roll call, each man,
"Ad sum," the present is never entombed,
Kai gar speaks for us the endless *Amen*.

STABAT MATER DOLOROSA

Stood the mother sad watch keeping,
Near the cross, o'erwhelmed in weeping,
With the suffering Son in view.
Tried her spirit, full of groaning,
Sore distressed and deeply moaning,
Grief's sharp sword had pierced it through.

O what sadness, what affliction,
On whom fell God's benediction,
Mother of the only Son!

She was wailing, deeply grieving,
And was filled with dread, perceiving
Pangs that hurt her noble One.

What man is there without weeping
Could behold Christ's mother steeping
Her soul in that sore distress?
Who would not be wrung with anguish,
Seeing that fond mother languish
While her Son finds no redress?

For the sins of his elected
She saw Jesus now rejected,
'Neath the scourgings he must bear;
She beheld her child endearing,
Suffering, dying, no one nearing,
While he breathed his life out there.

Mother dear, fount of affection,
Let me feel thy sad dejection,
That I with thee grief may share;
Fill my heart with deep emotion,
Loving Christ in pure devotion,
Thus make me his consort there.

Grant, O Mother, this petition,
Fix his wounds without remission,
Fix them firmly in my heart;

Of thy Son now hurt with flaying,
All so worthy, for me praying,
Of the death pains give me part.

Let me join with thee in sorrow,
Something from the cross to borrow,
While I here my life shall live;
Near that cross my sad watch keeping,
Close companion in thy weeping,
To thy grief my soul I give.

Virgin of all virgins, glorious,
Pierce me not with look censorious,
Let me of thy sorrows share;
Make me know Messiah's dying,
Fellow sufferer with him crying,
And his stripes anew to bear.

Wound me deeply with the smiting,
All my soul the cross inviting,
While thy Son's love leads the way;
Then illumined, then transported,
May I, virgin, be supported
By thee on the Judgment day.

Let the cross guard me securely,
Christ in death defend me surely,
Nourished by his gracious care;

When my soul from death is fleeing,
Grant that all my ransomed being
Glorious Paradise may share.

OUR MOTHER'S SONG

I COULD not get to sing
Until to-day the song
That in my heart was born
The day our mother died.

I dare not sing it now,
That heart-song born of grief;
I wait till all my soul
Its sure relief shall find.

But I am near in thought
The sweet celestial place,
The blessed region where
The saintly anthems rise.

I cannot note them all,
Those pure harmonious strains;
I wait to learn them well
When sin's harsh notes are still.

But yet I list to hear
Above earth's discords loud
What spirits whisper low
When sometime hovering near.

I turn my inmost ear
And earth sounds die away;
I hear, and know I hear,
The song our mother sings.

"Home, home, sweet home, O Christ!"
This is her own dear hymn;
And where with Thee she sings,
Be there our home and song.

Im TheStory

personalised classic books

JANE
IN
WONDERLAND

LEWIS
CARROLL

"Beautiful gift.. lovely finish,
My Niece loves it, so precious!"

Helen R Brumfieldon

★★★★★

UNIQUE
GIFT

FOR KIDS, PARTNERS
AND FRIENDS

Timeless books such as:

Kids

Alice in Wonderland · The Jungle Book · The Wonderful Wizard of Oz
Peter and Wendy · Robin Hood · The Prince and The Pauper
The Railway Children · Treasure Island · A Christmas Carol

Adults

Romeo and Juliet · Dracula

Highly
Customizable

Change
Books Title

Replace
Characters Names
with yours

Upload
photo for
inside page!

Add
Inscriptions

Visit
Im TheStory .com
and order yours today!

CPSIA information can be obtained
at www.ICGtesting.com
Printed in the USA
BVHW041152160819
556068BV00023B/2696/P